REASONABLE G

A FEW GOOD REASONS WHY GOD

CW01496339

By Paul Lyndon B........,

BAHons, PGCE, QTS

Other Books by the same Author

Your 7 Days To Joy

Pray Like The Boss

The Antichrist Endgame

Your Time To Shine

I Am Who He Says I Am

The Secret Messiah

Available to buy now on Amazon

www.amazon.com

www.amazon.co.uk

DEDICATION

To every budding Apologist.

"...because that which is known of God is revealed in them, for God revealed it to them. For the invisible things of him since the creation of the world are clearly seen, being perceived through the things that are made, even his everlasting power and divinity, that they may be without excuse."
Romans 1:19-20

"In the beginning, God created the heavens and the earth."
Genesis 1:1

CONTENTS

REASONABLE GOD

A FEW GOOD REASONS WHY GOD EXISTS

PREFACE

It is with great pleasure that I introduce this concise work, '*Reasonable God, a few good reasons why God exists.*' In the pages that follow, I attempt to embark on an enlightening journey into the realm of Christian apologetics, presenting a compelling case for theistic rationality and coherence.

In an era marked by skepticism and intellectual challenges to religious belief, it is imperative to engage in thoughtful dialogue and provide cogent reasons for the claims we make. This book serves as an excellent introduction to Christian apologetics, shedding light on the fundamental questions that have intrigued and perplexed humanity for centuries.

This short work encompasses a range of topics central to Christian apologetics. From the nature of nothing and the cosmological argument to the nature of God, the fine-tuning argument, objective morality, and free will, I attempt to navigate through these intricate concepts with clarity and intellectual rigour. I hope to demonstrate a commendable ability to distill complex ideas into concise and accessible explanations, making this book an ideal starting point for those seeking an introduction to these crucial aspects of Christian thought.

My constant approach is one that embraces both reason and faith, recognising the compatibility between intellectual inquiry and heartfelt conviction. Throughout these pages, readers will find an emphasis on the integration of faith and reason, with each chapter building upon the previous ones to form a comprehensive and coherent case for the rationality of Christian belief.

This book does not seek to provide a comprehensive treatise on every facet of Christian apologetics. Instead, it serves as a springboard for further exploration and deeper engagement with the subjects it covers. Therefore I invite you to embark on your own intellectual journey, encouraging you to delve into the vast reservoir of Christian apologetics and to wrestle with the profound questions that lie at the intersection of faith and reason.

It is my hope that Reasonable God will inspire and equip readers to engage in thoughtful discussions about the Christian worldview. Whether you are a skeptic searching for answers, a seeker of truth, or a believer seeking to articulate your faith more effectively, I believe this book will provide you with a solid foundation and a compelling framework from which to embark on your own exploration of Christian apologetics.

May the ideas presented within these pages challenge your thinking, deepen your faith, and ignite a passion for understanding and sharing the reasons why God makes sense. Let us embark on this journey together, embracing the beauty of truth and the joy of discovery. So as you read this work take your time, read slowly and look up any words or definitions you do not understand. As you devote yourself to this study of apologetics, you will be richly rewarded with the knowledge of the Divine.

May God bless You as you read this book.
Paul Lyndon Burtwell.

Chapter One

OUT OF NOTHING, NOTHING COMES

In our quest to explore the evidence for the existence of God, we encounter a fundamental question: can something truly emerge from nothing? This chapter delves into the philosophical analysis that reveals the inherent impossibility of nothingness giving rise to something. Drawing inspiration from the works of esteemed philosophers, we will examine how the concept of nothingness lacks essential properties and powers, making it incapable of producing the universe.

The Lack of Properties and Potential

To comprehend the impossibility of nothing creating something, we must first understand the nature of nothingness itself. Nothingness refers to the complete absence of anything—no matter, energy, space, or even abstract concepts. It is an utter void, devoid of any properties or potential. Nothing is literally no-thing.

As someone once said, "Nothing is what rocks dream about all the day long!"

Nothingness lacks all properties because properties are inherent characteristics that define an entity. They describe what an object is, how it behaves, or what it can do. Since nothingness possesses no attributes whatsoever, it cannot possess the potential to generate anything.

Moreover, potentiality is intimately linked to properties. Potentiality refers to the capacity for an entity to possess certain properties or abilities. It implies that something has the ability to manifest certain characteristics or bring about specific effects. Yet, nothingness lacks all potentiality because it lacks all properties. Without properties, there can be no potential for anything to arise.

The Absence of Possibility and Power

In addition to lacking properties and potential, nothingness also lacks possibility and power. Possibility refers to the capacity for something to exist or occur. It entails the realm of feasible outcomes within the boundaries of logical coherence and metaphysical constraints. However, since nothingness lacks any properties, it cannot contain possibilities within itself. Without inherent properties or potential, the notion of possibility becomes utterly foreign to nothingness.

Furthermore, power is an essential aspect of causality —the capacity to bring about an effect. Power implies the ability to act and produce change. Nothingness, being devoid of any properties, potential, and possibilities, lacks the power to cause anything to come into existence. It is impotent, incapable of initiating or generating anything.

The Necessity of a Self-Existent Something

From our analysis, it becomes evident that nothingness, by its very nature, cannot be the cause of the universe. The absence of properties, potential, possibilities, and power renders nothingness impotent in the act of creation. If nothing cannot produce something, then we are left with only one logical conclusion: something must have brought the universe into existence.

This something, which possesses the necessary properties, potential, possibility, and power to create, cannot itself be contingent or dependent on something else. It must be self-existent, existing necessarily and eternally. By virtue of its self-existence, this something stands beyond the limitations of time, space, and causality. It transcends the boundaries of the universe and becomes the foundation of all that exists.

Conclusion

In exploring the concept of nothingness and its inability to generate something, we have arrived at a profound realisation. The evidence firmly points towards the necessity of a self-existent something — a transcendent, eternal entity — as the cause of the universe. This something possesses the properties, potential, possibilities, and power required for creation, in stark contrast to the inherent limitations of nothingness.

As we continue our investigation into the evidence for the existence of God, we shall delve further into the nature of this self-existent something. We shall explore various philosophical arguments and engage with scientific insights to deepen our understanding and affirm the existence of a powerful, eternal Creator.

A Simplified Summary

This chapter is all about whether something can come from nothing, and it explains why it's impossible. When we talk about nothingness, we mean a complete absence of anything—no stuff, no energy, and even no ideas. It's like an empty space with absolutely nothing in it - including that space!

Nothingness doesn't have any properties or potential because those things describe what something is or what it can do. Since nothingness doesn't have any of these qualities, it can't create, produce or make anything. It's like a blank sheet of paper that can't draw or write upon itself.

Nothingness also doesn't have any possibilities or power. Possibility means something can exist or happen, but since nothingness has no properties, it can't contain any possibilities. Power means the ability to do things and make changes, but nothingness doesn't have any power because it has no properties or potential.

Because of all these reasons, we can see that nothingness can't be the reason why the universe exists. It can't create anything because it doesn't have any properties, potential, possibilities, or power to do so. So, we need to think about something else that could have created the universe.

This something must be self-existent, which means it exists by itself and doesn't depend on anything else. It must have the properties, potential, possibilities, and power to create everything we see. It's like a super powerful and eternal being that is beyond our understanding of time, space and matter.

To sum it up, when we look at the idea of nothingness, we see that it can't create something. So, it makes far more sense to believe in a powerful and eternal Creator who has the ability to create the universe.

Study Questions

Q1: What does "nothingness" mean in the context of this argument? Explain why nothingness lacks properties and potential.

Q2: Why is it important for something to have properties and potential in order to create or produce something else?

Q3: What does the concept of "possibility" mean? How does the absence of properties in nothingness affect its capacity for possibility?

Q4: What does the argument say about the power of nothingness? Why is power important in the act of creation?

Q5. According to the argument, why is a self-existent something necessary to explain the existence of the universe? What qualities must this self-existent something possess?

Chapter Two

IN THE BEGINNING

In our pursuit of understanding the evidence for the existence of God, we encounter the powerful reasoning of the Kalam Cosmological Argument. Developed by philosophers and theologians throughout history, this argument provides a compelling case for the existence of a transcendent cause of the universe. In this chapter, we will explore the argument's two premises, analyse their significance, and arrive at the compelling conclusion that the universe indeed has a cause. The Kalam Cosmological argument can be formulated like this:

Premise 1: Everything That Begins to Exist Has a Cause

Premise 2: The Universe Began to Exist.

Conclusion: The Universe Has a Cause.

Let us now take a look to see if this argument is sound.

Premise 1: Everything That Begins to Exist Has a Cause

The first premise of the Kalam Cosmological Argument states that everything that begins to exist has a cause. This principle finds support in our everyday experience and our understanding of causality. We observe that objects, events, and phenomena in the natural world have identifiable causes that bring them into existence or initiate their occurrence.

Consider, for instance, the construction of a building. Before the building exists, it requires architects, engineers, builders, and construction materials. These causes work together, bringing about the construction of the building. We intuitively recognise that temporal things do not come into existence from nothing; they have causes that precede their existence.

Premise 2: The Universe Began to Exist

The second premise of the Kalam Cosmological Argument asserts that the universe began to exist. This premise aligns with scientific discoveries and philosophical reasoning about the nature of time and space. Overwhelming evidence from cosmology, such as the Big Bang theory, points to a finite history of the universe, implying a moment when it came into existence.

Scientists have observed that the universe is expanding, which means that if we trace back its expansion, we eventually reach a point of singularity— an initial moment of the universe's existence. This realisation supports the notion that the universe had a beginning, a moment when it transitioned from non-existence to existence.

The Borde-Guth-Vilenkin (BGV) theorem, offers further support for the notion of an absolute beginning of the universe. Named after its discoverers, Arvind Borde, Alan Guth, and Alexander Vilenkin, this theorem demonstrates that any universe which has, on average, been expanding throughout its history cannot be eternal in the past but must have a finite beginning. The BGV theorem relies on a combination of general relativity and an understanding of cosmic expansion. By considering the properties of cosmic time and the rate of expansion, the theorem reveals that a universe with an average expansion rate greater than zero cannot extend infinitely into the past but must have a definite starting point. This theorem adds significant weight to the conclusion that our universe had an absolute beginning, providing further evidence for the existence of a transcendent cause that initiated its existence. As Alexander Vilenkin affirms,

"It is said that an argument is what convinces reasonable men and a proof is what it takes to convince even an unreasonable man. With the proof now in place, cosmologists can no longer hide behind the possibility of a past-eternal universe. There is no escape: they have to face the problem of a cosmic beginning."

Conclusion: The Universe Has a Cause

By accepting both premises of the Kalam Cosmological Argument, we are compelled to draw the logical conclusion that the universe has a cause. Premise 1 establishes the principle that everything that begins to exist requires a cause, and Premise 2 affirms that the universe began to exist. When we combine these premises, we find that the universe must have a cause that brought it into existence.

This conclusion has profound implications. It leads us to contemplate the existence of a transcendent, uncaused cause beyond the physical realm—a cause that is timeless, spaceless, immaterial and powerful enough to initiate the universe's existence. This cause, therefore becomes the ultimate explanation for the origin and existence of the universe.

In the subsequent chapters, we shall explore additional philosophical and scientific insights that further bolster the case for the existence of this transcendent cause. We shall delve into the intricate details of cosmology, metaphysics, and theology, uncovering a rich tapestry of evidence that points us towards the reality of a purposeful Creator.

A Simplified Summary

In our journey to understand if God exists, we come across a powerful argument called the Kalam Cosmological Argument. It has two important ideas that lead us to believe that the universe has a cause. The first idea is that everything that begins to exist has a cause. We see this in our everyday lives, where things are made by someone or something. The second idea is that the universe began to exist. Scientists have discovered that the universe had a starting point, called the Big Bang. This means that the universe didn't always exist but had a moment when it began. By combining these two ideas, we can conclude that the universe must have a cause that brought it into existence. This cause is something beyond the physical world, something timeless, spaceless, immaterial, and powerful. It points us to the existence of a Creator who made the universe.

Study Questions

Q1: What is the first premise of the Kalam Cosmological Argument?

Hint: It states that everything that begins to exist has a _____.

Q2: Give an example from everyday life that supports the first premise.

Hint: Think about something that is made or created.

Q3: What does the second premise of the Kalam Cosmological Argument assert about the universe?

Hint: It states that the universe _____ to exist.

Q4: What scientific theory provides evidence for the beginning of the universe?

Hint: It's often condensed to three capital letters _____.

Q5: What does the conclusion of the Kalam Cosmological Argument tell us about the universe?

Hint: It suggests that the universe has a _____.

Chapter Three

THE NATURE OF THE CAUSE

As we delve deeper into the evidence for the existence of a first cause of the universe, we must explore the profound nature of this transcendent entity. This chapter unravels the characteristics of the first cause that extend beyond the limitations of space, time, and matter. We will examine its spaceless, timeless, and immaterial nature, its causal priority, and the presence of will that allowed it to bring the universe into being.

The First Cause: Beyond Space, Time, and Matter

To comprehend the nature of the first cause, we must recognise that it stands apart from the very fabric of the universe it brought into existence. As the cause of space, time, and matter, it cannot itself be confined by these entities. Instead, it transcends them.

Being spaceless, the first cause exists independent of any spatial constraints. It does not occupy a particular location within the universe, for it precedes the existence of space itself. Similarly, being timeless, it exists without being subject to the flow of time. It stands outside the temporal dimension, beyond the sequential progression we experience within the universe.

Moreover, the first cause is immaterial. It lacks a physical form or composition, as it predates the emergence of matter. It exists in a realm beyond the physical, operating on a different ontological plane.

Causality and Transcendent Existence

The first cause, by its very nature, exists causally prior to the universe. It is the originating force that brought space, time, and matter into being. Since the universe is contingent and dependent, it requires a cause that transcends its own existence. The first cause, being the source of all causality within the universe, must itself exist causally prior to it.

Furthermore, the first cause possesses the power and potential necessary to bring the universe into existence. Its potency far surpasses anything within the physical realm. It possesses the ability to initiate and sustain the universe, infusing it with the fundamental properties and laws that govern its existence.

The Will to Create

In addition to its transcendent nature and causal priority, the first cause exhibits a volitional aspect—an intentional will to create. This will distinguishes it from being a mere impersonal force or a mechanical process. It possesses the conscious agency to make a deliberate decision to bring the universe into existence. This volitional aspect of its nature also explains how a temporal effect (the universe) can arise from an eternal cause.

The presence of will is particularly significant, as it implies a purpose behind the act of creation. The first cause, with its conscious volition, can shape the course of events and imbue the universe with intentionality and design.

Conclusion

In contemplating the nature of the first cause, we encounter a profound entity that transcends the limitations of space, time, and matter. It exists as a spaceless, timeless, and immaterial entity, possessing the power and potential to initiate and sustain the universe. As the causal source of the universe, it stands causally prior to it, while its will to create infuses purpose and intentionality into the fabric of the cosmos. In the subsequent chapters, we will further explore the implications of these characteristics, delving into philosophical and theological arguments that shed light on the nature and attributes of the first cause. Our journey of understanding will deepen, revealing a remarkable Creator whose existence is supported by a compelling array of evidence and reasoning.

A Simplified Summary

This chapter talks about a special thing called the "first cause" that started the whole universe. This first cause is different from everything else because it exists beyond space, time, and matter. It doesn't have a specific place, it is not limited by time, and it doesn't have a physical form like we do. It is also the reason why everything in the universe exists. The first cause has the power to create and sustain the universe, and it made a personal choice to bring it into existence. This means that there is a purpose and intention behind everything we see in the world.

Study Questions

Q1: What are three characteristics of the first cause that set it apart from everything else in the universe?

Q2: Why is the first cause described as spaceless, timeless, and immaterial?

Q3: What does it mean for the first cause to exist 'causally' prior to the universe?

Q4: What is the significance of the first cause having a will to create?

Q5: How does the presence of will in the first cause imply purpose and intentionality in the creation of the universe?

Chapter Four

WHY NOT AN ETERNAL UNIVERSE?

In our exploration of the evidence for the existence of a first cause, we encounter a compelling argument against the notion of an eternal universe composed of an actual infinite regress of temporal past events. Utilising the classic example of *Hilbert's Hotel*, we can vividly illustrate the absurdities that arise when we consider the existence of an infinite chain of past events in an eternal universe. This chapter examines the impossibility of actual infinites in reality and distinguishes them from potential infinities that might extend into the future.

Hilbert's Hotel: Unveiling the Absurdities of Actual Infinities

The Hilbert's Hotel thought experiment, formulated by the mathematician David Hilbert, provides a powerful illustration of the contradictions inherent in an actual infinite regress. To begin, imagine a hotel with an infinite number of rooms, all of which are fully occupied. Now, suppose a new guest arrives and requests a room. Surprisingly, the hotel manager claims to accommodate the new guest by shifting each occupant to the room with a number twice their current room number (i.e., the guest in Room 1 moves to Room 2, the guest in Room 2 moves to Room 4, and so on). Remarkably, despite the infinite number of already existing guests, and a fully occupied hotel, there is now an available room for the new arrival!

This paradoxical scenario demonstrates the counterintuitive nature of actual infinites. It reveals that manipulating an infinite series of events can lead to nonsensical outcomes. The existence of an actual infinite chain of past events such as seconds, hours, days, weeks or years would raise similar paradoxes, challenging the coherence and logical consistency of such a scenario. As such there could not have been an infinite number of days prior to today and therefore the universe is not eternal in nature.

Potential Infinities and Future Possibilities

While actual infinites are fraught with contradictions, potential infinities hold a different character. We can conceive of potential infinities extending into the future, where events or possibilities continue indefinitely. For instance, we can imagine the future possibility of counting to arbitrarily large numbers without end by simply adding one more number. However, it is crucial to note that potential infinities are not actualised in reality; they remain conceptual and theoretical constructs.

The Fallacy of Equating Potential and Actual Infinities

Therefore it is a fallacy to assume that potential infinities provide evidence for the existence of an actual infinite regress of past events. Potential infinities extending into the future do not overcome the inherent contradictions associated with actual infinites. They merely represent an unbounded realm of possibilities without traversing an infinite chain of events. The potential for future events to continue indefinitely does not establish the viability of an actual infinite regress in the past.

The Impossibility of an Actual Infinite Regress

From Hilbert's Hotel to logical paradoxes, the impossibility of an actual infinite regress becomes evident. The contradictions and absurdities that arise when dealing with actual infinites highlight their incompatibility with the nature of reality. Thus, it becomes implausible to argue that an infinite chain of past events could exist, necessitating a timeless first cause that transcends the limitations of infinite regress.

Science Confirms a Beginning

In addition to the logical arguments against a past eternal universe, we now have strong confirmation from science. Here are four examples:

1. Second Law of Thermodynamics:
The second law of thermodynamics tells us that energy tends to spread out and become less organised over time. If the universe had been here forever, all the energy would have spread out and become unusable by now. But we still see organised and useful energy around us, like sunlight, starlight and electricity, which means the universe hasn't been here forever.

2. Expansion of the Universe:
Scientists have discovered that the universe is expanding, which means it is getting bigger over time.

If the universe had always existed, it would have already reached maximum expansion, and everything would be very spread out. But we can still see galaxies close together, so the universe must have had a beginning.

3. Cosmic Microwave Background Radiation:
Scientists have detected a faint glow of radiation called the cosmic microwave background. This radiation is leftover from the early stages of the universe, and it helps us understand its history. If the universe had no beginning and was past eternal, this radiation would have spread out completely and become undetectable. But we can still observe it, which tells us that the universe had a starting point.

4. Big Bang Theory:
The Big Bang theory is the scientific explanation for the origin of the universe. It suggests that the universe began from an incredibly hot and dense state about 13.8 billion years ago. Many observations and

experiments support this theory, providing strong evidence that the universe had a definite beginning.

So, when we consider the stars are still shining, the second law of thermodynamics, the expansion of the universe, the cosmic microwave background radiation, and the Big Bang theory, we find compelling reasons why the universe cannot be past eternal. It had a definite beginning, and it has been expanding, changing and evolving since then.

Conclusion

In examining the impossibility of an actual infinite regress, we have encountered Hilbert's Hotel and witnessed the logical absurdities that arise when dealing with actual infinites. While potential infinities may exist as conceptual possibilities, they do not lend support to the idea of an actual infinite regress in the past. The logical and scientific evidence points us towards the need for a first cause that breaks the chain of regress and establishes the origin of temporal events. As we delve further into our exploration, we will uncover additional arguments and insights that illuminate the existence of a transcendent Creator, independent of an infinite regress of temporal past events.

A Simplified Summary

Hilbert's strange hotel scenario helps us understand why an infinite chain of past events is not possible. It shows that dealing with actual infinities can lead to confusing and nonsensical situations. If the universe had an infinite number of past days, similar paradoxes would arise, and it would not make sense. Therefore, the universe cannot have existed forever.

However, we can still think about the future having endless possibilities or events that continue forever. For example, we can imagine counting to larger and larger numbers without ever stopping simply by adding another number: 100… 101…102… and so on. But it's important to know that these future possibilities are just ideas and not something that actually happens in reality.

So, while it's okay to think about never-ending things in the future, we cannot use that to prove that there was an infinite chain of events in the past. The contradictions and problems that come with actual infinites show that it's impossible for the universe to have existed forever. Instead, there must have been a timeless first cause that started everything.

Science also supports the idea that the universe had a beginning. The second law of thermodynamics tells us that energy spreads out and becomes less organised over time. If the universe had been here forever, all the energy would have spread out completely by now. But we still see organised energy around us, like sunlight, starlight and electricity. The expansion of the universe and the presence of cosmic microwave background radiation also tell us that the universe started at a specific point in time.

All these pieces of evidence from science, along with the logical arguments, lead us to believe that the universe had a beginning and has been expanding since then. The idea of an infinite chain of past events doesn't make sense when we consider these facts. So, there must be a first cause, a creator that exists independently of the universe's finite past.

Study Questions

Q1: What is Hilbert's Hotel, and how does it help illustrate the problems with an infinite chain of past events?

Q2: Explain the difference between actual infinities and potential infinities, and why potential infinities do not support the idea of an infinite regress of events in the past.

Q3: What are some scientific examples that support the idea of the universe having a beginning?

Q4: How does the second law of thermodynamics contradict the idea of a past eternal universe?

Q5: What is the Big Bang theory, and how does it provide evidence for the universe having a definite starting point?

Chapter Five

THE PRIME MOVER

In this chapter, we will explore one of the foundational arguments for the existence of God, namely the necessity of a Prime Mover. The idea of a Prime Mover finds its roots in ancient philosophical thought, but it has found renewed interest and support in contemporary Christian apologetics. Drawing inspiration from the writings of philosophers past and present, we will present a compelling case for the existence of a Prime Mover and its implications for understanding the nature of God.

The Argument from Change

The starting point of our argument lies in the observation of change in the world around us. It is evident that objects and events undergo transformations from one state to another. However, it is important to recognise that change cannot be infinitely regressive. If we trace the series of changes backward, we eventually reach a point where change must have been initiated by something unchanging or what could be called, the Prime Mover.

The Causality Principle

The principle of causality, often referred to as the law of cause and effect, supports the existence of a Prime Mover. Every event or change has a cause, which necessitates a chain of causality. However, this chain cannot extend infinitely into the past, for an infinite regress of causes is logically untenable. Therefore, there must be a first cause—a necessary being—who sets the entire causal chain in motion. This first cause, or Prime Mover, is uncaused and self-existent.

The Nature of the Prime Mover

What can we ascertain about the nature of this Prime Mover? By examining the characteristics required for a necessary being, we can draw several conclusions. Firstly, the Prime Mover must exist outside the natural realm since it is not subject to the laws of causality within it. Secondly, the Prime Mover must be timeless and eternal, for it is not bound by the constraints of temporal existence. Thirdly, the Prime Mover must possess immense power and intelligence to initiate and sustain the entire cosmos.

Implications for God's Existence

The identification of the Prime Mover as a necessary being carries significant theological implications. It aligns with the Judeo-Christian concept of God as the First Cause, the unmoved mover, and the creator of the universe. The Prime Mover's transcendence over natural causality points to the supernatural nature of God, who exists beyond the physical world.

Furthermore, the Prime Mover's timeless and eternal nature resonates with the biblical understanding of God as the Alpha and the Omega, the beginning and the end.

Response to Objections

Critics may argue that positing a Prime Mover is an unnecessary assumption or a God-of-the-gaps explanation. However, such objections overlook the logical necessity of a first cause and fail to provide an alternative explanation for the origin of change and causality. Additionally, skeptics might question the nature of the Prime Mover or inquire into its attributes. While these questions remain open to further exploration, they do not undermine the central argument for the necessity of a Prime Mover as a foundational principle.

Conclusion

The concept of a Prime Mover presents a compelling argument for the existence of God. Through logical and philosophical reasoning, we have demonstrated the necessity of a first cause—an unchanging, self-existent, and transcendent entity. This Prime Mover aligns with the characteristics ascribed to the God of Christianity and points towards a deeper understanding of God's nature. By embracing the notion of a Prime Mover, we gain insight into the divine origin and sustaining power behind the universe we inhabit.

A Simplified Summary

In this chapter, we talked about why many people believe that God exists, from an argument called the Prime Mover. We understand that everything in the world is always changing, but there must be something that started all the changes. This thing is called the Prime Mover. We also understand that every change has a cause, but there can't be an infinite number of causes because that doesn't make logical sense. So there must be a first cause, which is the Prime Mover. Therefore we can conclude that the Prime Mover exists outside of our world, is very powerful and smart, and has always been there. This idea matches what Christians believe about God, that He created everything and has always existed. Some people might disagree and say we don't need to believe in a Prime Mover, but they haven't explained how everything started and what initiated change. While there are still questions about the Prime Mover, this argument shows why many people think God exists and why He is important.

Study Questions

Q1: What is the main idea behind the argument of the Prime Mover?

Q2: Why is it important to recognise that change cannot go on forever?

Q3: What does the principle of causality tell us about the existence of a Prime Mover?

Q4: What are some characteristics of the Prime Mover as discussed in this chapter?

Q5: How does the concept of the Prime Mover relate to the belief in God according to the Christian faith?

Chapter Six

THE FINE TUNER

In this chapter, we will delve into the fascinating concept of fine-tuning and its implications for the existence of a Fine Tuner—a powerful argument in support of God's existence. This argument asserts that the laws, parameters and conditions of the universe are precisely fine-tuned to allow the existence of intelligent life, implying the presence of an intelligent designer, often associated with God. Here we will explore six of the many compelling examples of fine-tuning in the universe, each with its specific fine-tuning parameter, and discuss why design is the only viable explanation for this intricate balance.

The Cosmological Constant

The fine-tuning parameter for the Cosmological Constant is estimated to be on the order of 1 in 10^120. This extraordinarily precise value allows the expansion rate of the universe to be finely balanced, allowing for the emergence of a universe fit for life.

To help put this parameter into perspective imagine a scale with a needle positioned precisely in the middle, with the width of the range being 1 in 10^120. An infinitesimal adjustment in either direction would disrupt the delicate equilibrium required for our universe.

In other words if the Cosmological Constant were to vary by 1 part in

10,000,000,000,000,000,000,000,000,000,000,000,000 ,000,000,000,000,000,000,000,000,000,000,000,000,0 00,000,000,000,000,000,000,000,000,000,000,000,000 ,000,000,000,000,000,000,000,000,000,000,000,000,0 00,000,000, we would cease to exist.

To help illustrate this further, imagine you have been blindfolded and set the following task. On your first attempt you are required to pick out a single, specific marked grain of sand buried somewhere in the beaches of the world. But here's the catch, if you pick out the wrong grain of sand the universe will cease to exist along with everyone in it!

The probability that you will pick the correct grain of sand on your first attempt is 1 chance in 10^{19}. Or 1 chance in 10,000,000,000,000,000,000.

A very small chance indeed! However, this chance is exceedingly greater than that for the fine tuning of the Cosmological Constant at 1 in 10^{120}. This simple illustration helps us understand how incredibly fine tuned the laws of nature need to be for our existence.

Gravitational Force

The strength of the gravitational force is fine-tuned to an astonishing degree, with a parameter of approximately 1 in 10^{40}. This precise calibration permits stable planetary orbits, the formation of galaxies, and the conditions necessary for life to exist.

Strong and Weak Nuclear Forces

The strength of the strong nuclear force, with a fine-tuning parameter of roughly 1 in 10^38, and the weak nuclear force, with a parameter of about 1 in 10^45, must be finely balanced. These forces govern the stability of atomic nuclei and the occurrence of radioactive decay, without which life as we know it would not be possible.

Electromagnetic Force

The electromagnetic force is fine-tuned with a parameter of approximately 1 in 10^40. This precise calibration determines the behaviour of charged particles, governs the interactions of atoms and molecules, and enables the chemical reactions necessary for life.

Ratio of Electrons to Protons

The ratio of electrons to protons in the universe is fine-tuned with a parameter estimated to be on the order of 1 in 10^37. This delicate balance ensures electrical neutrality, allowing the formation of atoms, molecules, and the complexity necessary for life.

Carbon Resonance Levels

The resonance levels of the carbon atom are fine-tuned with a parameter of approximately 1 in 10^40. This precise calibration enables the synthesis of complex organic molecules necessary for life and the chemistry that sustains it.

In contemplating the remarkable fine-tuning of the universe, one encounters a profound question: What could possibly account for this intricate balance of physical constants and initial conditions that permit the existence of intelligent life? The options at hand are three: chance, necessity, or design. Let us delve into each possibility, examining their plausibility in light of the overwhelming evidence.

Chance

Firstly, chance suggests that the universe's exquisite fine-tuning is merely a product of happenstance. However, the sheer magnitude of the probabilities stacked against this notion is staggering. The range of possible values for the fundamental constants and initial conditions is astronomically vast, and yet the finely-tuned values required for life to arise are incredibly narrow. The odds of such an outcome occurring randomly are infinitesimally small, resembling a cosmic lottery where every ticket is a losing one. Therefore, the appeal to chance as an explanation for fine-tuning lacks credibility.

Necessity

Secondly, one might propose that the fine-tuning is a result of necessity, claiming that the universe must possess these precise parameters and conditions. Yet, such a position faces a formidable challenge. There is no inherent reason why the universe should have these particular values and configurations. There is no theoretical or empirical basis indicating that the constants of nature had to be precisely as they are. In fact, the delicate balance of the fundamental parameters seems to defy the notion of necessity. Thus, the argument from necessity fails to provide a compelling explanation for the finely-tuned nature of the universe.

Design

Finally, we turn to the third option: design. The intricate precision and specificity of the universe's fine-tuning suggest the handiwork of a purposeful Creator. The astonishing harmony of the fundamental constants and initial conditions, orchestrated with incredible finesse, indicates that the universe was intentionally crafted to allow for the emergence of intelligent life. The intricate interplay of forces, the delicate balance of energy, and the precise arrangement of matter all point towards an intelligent mind behind it all. The mathematical odds alone, combined with the absence of alternative explanations, bolster the case for design as the most plausible explanation for the fine-tuned parameters that are indispensable for the existence of our universe and the emergence of sentient beings.

Conclusion

In conclusion, we can formulate an argument for design like this,

Premise 1: The fine tuning of the laws and constants of nature are due to either chance, necessity or design.
Premise 2: They are not due to chance or necessity.
Conclusion: Therefore, they are due to design.

When we critically assess the options of chance, necessity, or design to account for the fine-tuning of the universe, it becomes apparent that design emerges as the most compelling and intellectually satisfying explanation. The vast improbability of chance, the absence of necessity, and the unmistakable fingerprints of intelligent craftsmanship all converge to affirm the presence of a transcendent Designer who has fashioned the cosmos in such a way that life, consciousness, and the opportunity for exploration and discovery can flourish. The fine-tuning of the universe is not a coincidence; it is a testament to the ingenuity and purpose inherent in its very fabric.

The select few of many examples of fine-tuning presented here, each with its specific fine-tuning parameter, offer compelling evidence for the existence of a Fine Tuner. The sheer improbability of such precise calibration, as indicated by the astronomical numbers involved, points towards intentional design rather than chance or necessity. The intricate balance required for life to exist and flourish suggests a purposeful and intelligent agency behind the universe. In embracing the concept of fine-tuning, we gain a deeper understanding of the exquisite craftsmanship and intentional design woven into the fabric of our existence.

A Simplified Summary

This chapter talks about something called "fine-tuning" in the universe and how it supports the idea that God exists. Fine-tuning means that everything in the universe is perfectly balanced, or dialled in just right for life to exist. The chapter gives examples of this fine-tuning.

For example, one example is the "cosmological constant." It's a fancy term that means the universe is expanding at just the right rate. If it expanded too fast or too slow, life couldn't exist. It's like balancing a needle on its end, if it moves even a little bit this way or that, the needle topples and there goes the balancing act.

Another example is the force of gravity. It's just right to keep planets in their orbits and allow galaxies to form. If gravity were just slightly different, everything would be chaotic and unstable.

There are also other forces, like the strong and weak nuclear forces, and the electromagnetic force. These forces have to be perfectly balanced for atoms to be stable and for chemical reactions to happen. Without them, life wouldn't be possible.

The chapter also talks about the ratio of electrons to protons in the universe and the resonance levels of carbon atoms. Both of these things have to be just right for life to exist.

Now, the chapter explores three possible explanations for this fine-tuning: chance, necessity, and design. Chance means it happened randomly, but the chances of that are extremely tiny. It's like trying to find one specific grain of sand on all the beaches in the world blindfolded. The probability is so small, it's virtually impossible.

Necessity means it had to be this way, but there's no reason to think the universe had to be fine-tuned. There's no proof or theory saying it had to happen this way.

The last explanation is design, which means someone intentionally made the universe this way. The fine-tuning is like a sign that points to a creator. The balance and precision in the universe show that there must be an intelligent mind behind it all.

When we look at all the options, chance and necessity don't really make sense. Design seems like the best explanation for why everything is so perfectly balanced. The universe shows that there's a purpose and intelligence behind it.

In conclusion, the fine-tuning of the universe is like a puzzle that points to a creator. The brief examples given in this chapter show how everything has to be just right for life to exist. The evidence therefore suggests that an intelligent designer made the universe this way on purpose. Understanding fine-tuning helps us see how amazing and purposeful our existence is.

Study Questions

Q1: What is fine-tuning in the universe, and why is it important for the existence of life?

Q2: Give one example of fine-tuning mentioned in the chapter and explain why it is crucial for life to exist.

Q3: What are the three possible explanations for the fine-tuning of the universe discussed in the chapter?

Q4: Why is the explanation of chance unlikely to account for the fine-tuning of the universe? Provide an analogy to help understand its improbability.

Q5: According to the chapter, why is design considered the most plausible explanation for the fine-tuning of the universe?

Chapter Seven

THE MORAL LAW GIVER

In this chapter, we delve into a profound question that has challenged philosophers and theologians throughout history: the nature and foundation of objective moral values. Many worldviews propose various explanations for morality, ranging from cultural relativism to subjective individualism. However, the concept of objective moral values, which hold that moral principles are true and binding regardless of personal opinions or societal customs, demands a transcendent source. In exploring this idea, we will argue that the existence of a transcendent lawgiver is not only philosophically coherent but also necessary to ground the objective moral values we intuitively recognise.

The Moral Landscape

Human beings possess an innate moral sense that guides our ethical judgments. We perceive certain actions as objectively right or wrong, regardless of cultural norms or personal preferences. This moral landscape, with its peaks of goodness and valleys of moral deprivation, is a universal aspect of our shared human experience. However, the existence of objective moral values within this landscape raises an important question: What is the ultimate foundation for these moral truths?

The Inadequacy of Naturalism

Naturalistic explanations, which assert that the physical universe is all that exists, struggle to provide a satisfactory account of objective moral values. Naturalism, by its very nature, limits reality to the material world and lacks an objective basis for morality beyond individual or societal preferences. If moral values are merely subjective or culturally constructed, they lose their binding force and become subject to arbitrary manipulation.

The Quest for an Objective Foundation

To establish a foundation for objective moral values, we must seek a source that transcends the contingent realm of human existence. This search leads us to consider the existence of a transcendent lawgiver, a being that possesses the attributes necessary to ground moral values objectively.

The Nature of a Transcendent Lawgiver

A transcendent lawgiver must possess certain attributes to ground objective moral values. First, this lawgiver must be transcendent in nature, existing beyond the physical universe, as objective moral values must derive from a source outside the material realm. Second, the lawgiver must be personal, for only a personal agent can will and prescribe moral obligations. Finally, the lawgiver must be the perfect good, serving as the standard against which all moral values are measured.

The Argument from Moral Ontology

One compelling argument for a transcendent lawgiver rests on the nature of moral values themselves. Objective moral values exhibit properties such as being transcendent, universal, and categorical, suggesting that they are grounded in a necessary and ultimate foundation—a foundation that can be reasonably identified as a transcendent lawgiver.

The Argument from Moral Obligation

Another powerful argument emerges from the realm of moral obligations. Objective moral values manifest as compelling moral obligations that transcend personal desires or cultural norms. To account for the binding nature of these obligations, we require a moral lawgiver whose authority surpasses human conventions.

The Moral Argument as a Cumulative Case

The necessity of a transcendent lawgiver to provide objective moral values adds to the cumulative case for the existence of God. When combined with other arguments, such as the cosmological or teleological arguments, the moral argument reinforces the plausibility of a transcendent, personal, and morally perfect God as the ultimate source of objective moral values.

Conclusion

In conclusion then we can formulate this argument as follows,

Premise 1: If God does not exist, then objective moral values and duties do not exist.

Premise 2: Objective moral values and duties do exist.

Conclusion: Therefore, God does exist.

In this chapter, we have explored the necessity of a transcendent lawgiver to ground objective moral values. The existence of objective moral values is best explained by a source beyond the naturalistic realm, a personal and morally perfect being who provides the ultimate foundation for our moral intuitions. Without this transcendent lawgiver, we are left with moral relativism or subjective arbitrariness, undermining the very fabric of our moral landscape. Therefore, the existence of a transcendent lawgiver serves as a robust explanation for the objective moral values we recognise and uphold in this world.

A Simplified Summary

This chapter was all about trying to understand why we have moral values and where they come from. People have different ideas about morality, like thinking it changes depending on culture or personal opinions. But some people believe that moral values are true for everyone, at every time, no matter what they think or where they come from. This idea says that there must be a special objective source for these moral values. In this chapter, we argue that this source is a powerful being who is outside our world and who sets the rules for what is right and wrong based upon its own nature. We explain why this makes sense and why it's important to have this source for our moral values. As C.S. Lewis observes,

"The very idea of freedom presupposes some objective moral law which overarches rulers and ruled alike… Unless we return to the crude and nursery-like belief in objective values, we perish."

Study Questions

Q1: What is the main question that philosophers and theologians have been trying to answer about moral values?

Q2: What is the difference between subjective and objective moral values?

Q3: Why do naturalistic explanations struggle to provide a satisfactory account of objective moral values?

Q4: What are the attributes that a transcendent lawgiver must possess to ground objective moral values?

Q5: How does the existence of objective moral values contribute to the argument for the existence of a transcendent, personal, and morally perfect God?

Chapter Eight

I THINK, THEREFORE...

We now examine the profound questions surrounding human free will and consciousness. These aspects of our existence are central to our understanding of personal agency and the nature of our conscious experiences. We will argue that the existence of God is necessary to provide a coherent and trustworthy foundation for human free will and consciousness. Without God, our thoughts and choices would be reduced to mere products of random chemical reactions and soulless matter, undermining their reliability and our ability to trust our own cognitive faculties.

The Mystery of Human Consciousness

Human consciousness is an extraordinary phenomenon that defies simple explanations. It encompasses our subjective awareness, thoughts, emotions, and experiences. While scientific research has shed light on the neural correlates of consciousness, it fails to fully explain the origin and nature of subjective awareness itself. This mystery calls for a deeper exploration into the metaphysical aspects of consciousness.

The Challenge of Naturalism

Naturalistic explanations attempt to reduce consciousness to physical processes in the brain, asserting that our thoughts and experiences are solely the result of random chemical reactions and material interactions. However, such reductionistic accounts fall short in explaining the qualitative and subjective aspects of consciousness. Furthermore, if consciousness is merely an emergent property of physical processes, it becomes difficult to account for the existence of free will and the reliability of our cognitive faculties. As C.S. Lewis elucidates,

"Supposing there was no intelligence behind the universe, no creative mind. In that case, nobody designed my brain for the purpose of thinking. It is merely that when the atoms inside my skull happen, for physical or chemical reasons, to arrange themselves in a certain way, this gives me, as a by-product, the sensation I call thought. But, if so, how can I trust my own thinking to be true? It's like upsetting a milk jug and hoping that the way it splashes itself will give you a map of London. But if I can't trust my own thinking, of course I can't trust the arguments leading to Atheism, and therefore have no reason to be an Atheist, or anything else. Unless I believe in God, I cannot believe in thought: so I can never use thought to disbelieve in God."

Free Will and Determinism

The concept of free will is intimately tied to our sense of personal agency and responsibility. If we are nothing more than biological machines governed solely by deterministic processes, our choices become illusory, and moral accountability becomes untenable. Determinism, which denies the existence of genuine free will, undermines the moral fabric of human society and renders notions of praise, blame, and personal responsibility meaningless.

The Necessary Grounding in God

To provide a coherent and trustworthy foundation for human free will and consciousness, we must turn to the existence of God. God, as a necessary and self-existent being, is not subject to the deterministic limitations of the natural world. Being outside the physical realm, God can bestow upon human beings the capacity for genuine free will and consciousness, transcending the limitations of deterministic processes.

God as the Source of Rationality

Rationality, our capacity for reason and logical thinking, is intimately connected to consciousness and free will. However, if our thoughts are merely the byproduct of random chemical reactions and soulless matter, we have no reason to trust their reliability. God, as the grounding for our rationality, provides a foundation for our cognitive faculties and the trustworthiness of our thoughts, ensuring that our reasoning is not merely a result of blind material processes.

The Implications of God's Creation

God's creation of human free will and consciousness has profound implications for our understanding of ourselves and the world around us. It affirms our inherent dignity as moral agents, capable of making meaningful choices and engaging in genuine relationships. Furthermore, it opens the door to the possibility of a personal relationship with God, as conscious beings who can seek and know their Creator.

Conclusion

In this chapter, we have explored the necessity of God's creation of human free will and consciousness. The existence of God provides a coherent and trustworthy foundation for our conscious experiences and the reality of our free will. Without God, our thoughts would be reduced to mere products of random chemical reactions, and our choices would lack genuine agency. By embracing the existence of God, we affirm the profound significance of our conscious lives and our ability to engage with the world as rational, free moral agents.

A Simplified Summary

Human consciousness is a really amazing thing that we don't fully understand yet. It includes our thoughts, feelings, and experiences. Some scientists say that consciousness is just a result of our brains and how they work chemically. But that doesn't explain everything. If our thoughts are just random chemical reactions, how can we trust them to be true? It's like spilling milk and hoping it will make a map of the city of London. Without something bigger than us, like God, our thoughts and choices wouldn't really mean anything. We wouldn't have real freedom to make decisions, and we wouldn't be responsible for our actions, good or evil. God gives us a strong foundation for our thoughts and choices. With God, we can trust our minds and know that we have the power to make meaningful choices. It also means that we can have a special relationship with God, who created us and knows us best. So, God's existence gives our lives objective purpose and meaning.

Study Questions

Q1: What is human consciousness, and why is it considered a mystery?

Q2: How do naturalistic explanations fall short in explaining consciousness and its subjective aspects?

Q3: According to C.S. Lewis, why is it difficult to trust our own thinking without the existence of God?

Q4: How does the concept of free will relate to our sense of personal agency and responsibility?

Q5: Why is the existence of God necessary to provide a coherent and trustworthy foundation for human free will and consciousness?

Chapter Nine

APPARENT DESIGN

In this chapter, we investigate the fascinating realm of the teleological argument, also known as the argument from design. This argument presents a powerful case for the existence of an intelligent Creator based on the apparent order, complexity, and purpose found in the universe. It asserts that the intricate design observed in the natural world, from the fine-tuning of physical constants to the complexity of living organisms, suggests the existence of an intelligent mind behind it all. By examining the remarkable interplay of elements, systems, and functions within nature, the teleological argument points to an intricate design that is best explained by the existence of a purposeful and intelligent Creator. Through the careful observation of the intricacies of the universe, we are led to contemplate the existence of an ultimate Designer who fashioned the cosmos with wisdom and intentionality.

Telos in the Living Cell

A clear example of the teleological argument can be seen in the interdependency of components in a living cell. Living cells are highly complex systems that need certain components to exist, survive, and replicate. They have a cell membrane that separates them from the outside, genetic material (DNA) that contains instructions for their functions, and metabolic processes to obtain energy and carry out tasks. Cells may also have specialised structures called organelles for specific functions. They produce proteins, which are vital for their structure and activities. Cells can reproduce through division, ensuring their continuation. Maintaining a stable internal environment (homeostasis) is also crucial. In summary, cells require a membrane, DNA, metabolism, organelles, protein synthesis, reproduction, and homeostasis for their existence and functioning.

Swedish Flat Packed Wardrobes

I am sure that at some point we have all been to a certain Swedish furniture store and bought a flat packed, self assemble item of furniture. In the showroom the item of furniture certainly looked appealing, however when we got the flat packed box home the daunting challenge of assembling the item suddenly dawned on us. Here, we can use the illustration of a flat packed wardrobe to think about what would be required on the early earth to construct the first living, self replicating cell. To simplify this illustration let's think about just five things that would be required for the wardrobe's assembly: 1. the lit room in which to build it, 2. the builder, 3. the instruction manual, 4. the materials, and 5. the builder's intention.

Building the Wardrobe

The Lit Room: Creating the Space

Imagine embarking on the task of assembling a flat pack wardrobe. Before the wardrobe can come into existence, there must be a lit room in which it is built and housed. Similarly, the existence of a living cell necessitates an environment that is conducive to its formation and functioning. Within the intricate framework of our universe, we find a delicate balance of physical constants and cosmic conditions that provide the necessary "room" for life to emerge. The precise values of factors such as gravity, electromagnetism, and the cosmological constant are finely tuned, pointing towards a purposeful arrangement designed to sustain life.

The Builder: Orchestrating Complexity

Assembling a flat pack wardrobe requires a skilled builder who possesses the necessary knowledge, expertise, and capabilities to bring the components together. In the cellular realm, we encounter an awe-inspiring builder—the intricate machinery of life itself. Within the living cell, an array of complex biological systems operates seamlessly, each component fulfilling a specific function while harmonising with others. The presence of intricate molecular machines, such as DNA replication machinery and protein synthesis systems, suggests the existence of an intelligent agent, intricately involved in the creation, assembly and orchestration of life's complexity.

The Instruction Manual: Guiding the Process

A flat pack wardrobe is accompanied by an instruction manual, providing guidance to the builder, enabling them to assemble the wardrobe correctly. In the cellular world, we discover an astonishing information repository—the genetic code of 6.4 Billion letters (base pairs). DNA, the molecule that carries this code, contains the instructions required for the construction and operation of living organisms. The intricate language of DNA, with its specific sequences and genetic information, serves as a blueprint that guides the development, growth, and functioning of every living cell. The existence of this complex and specified information within the cell points towards an intelligent source that authored the instruction manual of life.

The Materials: Building Blocks of Life

To assemble a flat pack wardrobe, one needs the necessary materials—the individual components such as the panels of wood, hinges, screws, handles and feet that come together to form the final product. Similarly, within the cell, we encounter an assortment of essential building blocks—proteins, lipids, carbohydrates, and nucleic acids. These intricate molecules provide the structural elements, energy sources, and information carriers necessary for life's processes. The precise arrangement and interplay of these molecules within the cell showcase an exquisite level of design, hinting at an intentional creator who provided the materials required for life to exist.

The Builder's Intention: Purposeful Assembly

Finally, assembling a flat pack wardrobe requires the intention or desire of the builder to engage in the construction process. In the teleological argument, we recognise the presence of intention within the cell—the purposeful nature of life itself. Living organisms exhibit remarkable complexity and functionality, finely adapted to their environments. The exquisite designs observed in the living world, from the intricate machinery within cells to the interconnected ecosystems of our planet, imply a grand plan and intention behind the assembly of life.

Now just think, if any one of these five things were missing, your Swedish wardrobe would not exist!

Conclusion

In conclusion, the complexity and sophistication of a self-replicating cell far surpass the intricacies involved in assembling a flat-packed wardrobe. While the assembly of a wardrobe requires a room, a builder, an instruction manual, materials, and the builder's intention, a living cell exhibits a level of intricacy that transcends mere human craftsmanship. The cell's components, processes, and systems work harmoniously together, displaying an astonishing level of organisation and purposeful design.

The teleological argument, which emphasises the apparent design and purpose found in the universe, becomes resoundingly clear when examining the complexity of a living cell. The remarkable organisation, interdependence, and functionality displayed within the cell point towards the existence of an intelligent Creator. The intricacies of a self-replicating cell, far surpassing the assembly of a wardrobe, strongly suggest that there is a transcendent and purposeful mind behind the intricately designed natural world we observe.

In light of the teleological argument, the existence of a self-replicating cell serves as a compelling testament to the existence of God. The precision, complexity, and purpose exhibited within the cell point towards an intelligent and intentional Creator who orchestrated life's remarkable design. As we marvel at the intricacies of a living cell, we are led to contemplate the existence of a grand Designer, guiding the course of life and the universe itself. The teleological argument provides a persuasive foundation for understanding and embracing the existence of God as the ultimate source of purpose, design, and meaning in our world.

A Simplified Summary

This chapter talks about something called the teleological argument, which is also known as the argument from design. It's all about how the order and complexity in the universe suggest that there is an intelligent Creator who made everything. One way to understand this is by looking at living cells, which are very complex systems. Cells have different parts that they need to survive and reproduce, like a cell membrane, DNA, and special structures called organelles. They also have processes to get energy and make proteins. All these things have to work together for the cell to function properly.

To help explain this, let's think about building a flat packed wardrobe. When we buy one, we need a few things to put it together: a room with light, a person to build it, instructions, materials, and the intention to build it. In a similar way, for the first living cell to exist, there had to be the right environment, like Earth, where it could form. It also has a kind of instruction manual called DNA, which tells the cell how to grow and function. The cell has the materials it needs, like proteins and other molecules, to do its job. The cell itself also requires a skilled builder because it has many complex parts that work together. And it seems like there is a clear purpose behind the design of the cell and all living things.

In conclusion, the teleological argument says that the complexity and design we see in living cells and other complex systems in the universe, point to the existence of a Creator. Cells are much more complex than building a wardrobe, and they show an incredible level of organisation and purpose. This suggests that there is a higher power or God who created everything with a specific plan in mind. When we look at the intricacies of a living cell, we can't help but wonder about the existence of a grand Designer who made the universe and everything in it.

Study Questions

Q1: What is the teleological argument also known as, and what does it suggest about the existence of a Creator?

Q2: Give an example of complexity and interdependence in nature that supports the teleological argument.

Q3: What are some of the essential components needed for a living cell to exist and function?

Q4: How does the example of building a flat packed wardrobe help us understand the complexity of a living cell?

Q5: What does the teleological argument tell us about the existence of a higher power or God and their role in creating the universe and living organisms?

Chapter Ten

INNATE DESIRE

In the pursuit of defending the Christian faith, we must not only engage with intellectual arguments and evidence but also address the profound longings and desires that reside within the human heart. One such argument that resonates with the deepest yearnings of our being is the Argument from Innate Desire. This argument, grounded in our internal longings and aspirations, provides a powerful case for the existence of God, the only object capable of satisfying our most profound desires. As C.S. Lewis writes,

"Creatures are not born with desires unless satisfaction for these desires exists. A baby feels hunger; well, there is such a thing as food. A dolphin wants to swim; well, there is such a thing as water. Men feel sexual desire; well, there is such a thing as sex. If I find in myself a desire which no experience in this world can satisfy, the most probable explanation is that I was made for another world."

In this chapter, we will explore the logic and implications of the Argument from Innate Desire.

The Formal Argument

The argument from innate desire can be formulated like this:

Premise 1. Every natural, innate desire in us corresponds to some real object that can satisfy that desire.

Premise 2. There exists within us a desire which no object in the natural world can satisfy.

Conclusion 1. Therefore there must exist an object outside the natural world to satisfy this desire.

Conclusion 2. This object is God.

Let us know take a look to see if this argument is sound.

Premise 1: Every natural, innate desire in us corresponds to some real object that can satisfy that desire.

Human beings possess an array of natural and innate desires, ranging from the desire for love and companionship to the desire for purpose and meaning. These desires are not mere whims or fleeting emotions; they are deeply ingrained within our nature. The first premise of the argument asserts that for every desire we experience, there exists an object in reality that can potentially fulfil that desire. We find evidence for this premise in our daily experiences and observations.

Consider the desire for sustenance. The natural hunger we feel corresponds to the existence of food, which can satisfy our physical need. The desire for knowledge finds its fulfilment in the pursuit of education and discovery. Even the desire for beauty can be satisfied through the appreciation of art, music, and the wonders of nature. These examples illustrate that our innate desires are not random or arbitrary but point to real objects in the world that can meet those desires.

Premise 2: There exists within us a desire which no object in the natural world can satisfy.

While many of our innate desires find fulfilment within the natural world, we are also acquainted with a distinct longing that seems to transcend the confines of our physical existence. This desire is not satisfied by any finite or temporal object or experience. It is a yearning for something greater, something eternal, beyond the natural order. We encounter this longing when we ponder the nature of ultimate reality, the purpose of our existence, and the meaning of life itself. This second premise acknowledges the presence of a desire that cannot be satisfied by any material or worldly entity. This desire points to an object that lies beyond the boundaries of the natural world, as it surpasses the limitations of what the natural realm can offer. Such a desire hints at the existence of a transcendent reality, a realm that can fulfil our deepest aspirations and provide ultimate satisfaction.

Conclusion 1: Therefore, there must exist an object outside the natural world to satisfy this desire.

Building upon the previous premises, we arrive at a compelling conclusion: there must exist an object beyond the natural world that can adequately satisfy the desire that eludes the natural order. Since every innate desire corresponds to an object that can fulfil it, and since there exists a desire that remains unfulfilled within the natural world, logic necessitates the existence of an object that lies outside the boundaries of nature.

This inference is not arbitrary or contrived but emerges naturally from our understanding of desire and its relation to reality. The existence of an object outside the natural world becomes a coherent and reasonable explanation for our innate longing that transcends earthly limitations.

Conclusion 2: This object is God.

The final step in the Argument from Innate Desire identifies the object that can adequately satisfy the longing beyond the natural world. In the Christian framework, this object is none other than God. By definition, God is the ultimate reality, the source of all being, and the foundation of purpose and meaning. God possesses the attributes necessary to fulfil our deepest desires: love, wisdom, and perfect goodness.

Moreover, the concept of God encompasses the characteristics that align with our innate longings, such as the desire for eternal life, justice, and the resolution of suffering. God provides the necessary framework to understand the coherence of our deepest aspirations and grants us hope that our longings can find ultimate fulfilment in Him.

Conclusion

The Argument from Innate Desire draws our attention to the profound longings that reside within us and reveals their significance in pointing towards a reality beyond the natural world. Our innate desires, which correspond to real objects in the natural order, find their ultimate fulfilment in God—the object that transcends the limits of the physical realm.

This argument invites us to reflect on the nature of our desires and consider their implications for the existence of a higher reality. By acknowledging the unfulfilled desire within us and recognising the logical necessity of an object that can satisfy it, we are led to the conclusion that God exists as the ultimate fulfilment of our deepest longings.

A Simplified Summary

The Argument from Innate Desire suggests that our natural desires, such as the longing for love, companionship, purpose, and meaning, are not random but point to real objects in the world that can fulfil them. However, there is a deeper desire within us that goes beyond what the natural world can offer—a yearning for something greater and everlasting. This unfulfilled desire indicates the existence of a reality outside our world, something transcendent that can satisfy our deepest aspirations. Therefore, it logically follows that there must be an object beyond the natural world that can fulfil this longing. In the Christian perspective, this object is God, who embodies the qualities needed to fulfil our deepest desires, including love, wisdom, and perfect goodness. God aligns with our innate longings for eternal life, justice, and an end to suffering. Thus, the Argument from Innate Desire leads us to the conclusion that God exists as the ultimate fulfilment of our deepest desires, providing hope and meaning beyond what the natural world can offer.

Study Questions

Q1: What does the Argument from Innate Desire suggest about our natural desires?

Q2: How does the argument explain the longing that goes beyond what the natural world can fulfil?

Q3: Why is it logical to conclude that there must be an object outside the natural world that can satisfy our unfulfilled desire?

Q4: In the Christian perspective, who is identified as the object that can fulfil our deepest desires?

Q5: What does the Argument from Innate Desire teach us about finding meaning and fulfilment beyond the natural world?

THE GOSPEL MESSAGE

Do you ever feel lost or like something is missing in your life?

Have you ever asked yourself if there is more to this world than just what we see?

The good news is that there is hope and purpose available to you, and it can be found through a relationship with Jesus Christ.

Do you know that God loves you a lot and wants you to be part of his family?

But everyone makes mistakes, and those mistakes are called sin.

Some examples of sin could be lying, stealing, or even misusing the name of God or Jesus.

Sin separates us from God and can't be fixed by ourselves.

God sent his Son, Jesus, to Earth to fix the problem of sin.

Jesus lived a perfect life and then died on the cross to take the punishment for our sins.

After three days, Jesus came back to life, defeating death.

If you trust in Jesus and ask for his forgiveness, you can have your sins forgiven and be reconciled with God.

This means you can have eternal life with God in heaven.

It's a free gift that God offers to us because of his love and kindness.

This message is a message of hope and the opportunity to have a personal relationship with God through faith in Jesus.

It can change your life and bring you peace and purpose.

If you want to accept the gift of salvation through Jesus, you can pray this simple prayer:

"Dear God, I know that I am a sinner and I am sorry for my sins.

I believe that Jesus is your son and that he died on the cross to take the punishment for my sins.

I want to turn away from my sins and follow you.

Please forgive me and give me eternal life.

I accept your gift of salvation.

Thank you for loving me.

In Jesus' name, Amen."

If you prayed this prayer and meant it in your heart, congratulations!

You have taken the first step in your journey with Jesus.

Here are some next steps you can take:

1. Find a Bible and start reading it. It is God's word and will help guide you on your journey. A good place to start are the Gospels of Matthew, Mark, Luke and John.

2. Find a church or Christian community to be a part of. They can offer you support and guidance as you grow in your faith.

3. Share your decision with someone you trust. This could be a friend, family member, or Pastor.

4. Consider getting baptised. This is a public declaration of your faith and a way to show others that you have decided to follow Jesus.

Remember, your relationship with God is a journey and it will take time to grow and mature.

Don't be afraid to ask for help or guidance along the way.

God is with you every step of the way and he will never leave you or forsake you.

LET'S STAY IN TOUCH!

If you enjoyed this book please be sure to leave a positive review and tell others about it.
For further resources sign up and subscribe to our social media channels:

FACEBOOK
Paul Lyndon

YOUTUBE
Paul Lyndon Burtwell

EMAIL
cleaspringchurch@gmail.com

Thank you for all of your kind support and prayers.

Your friend and servant,

Paul Lyndon Burtwell.

Printed in Great Britain
by Amazon

25810851R00066